Handwriting

+

Simple Sentences

Workbook

I like to run.

It is a sunny day.

I am amazing.

I sat on the mat.

This book belongs to:

____

Handwriting

+

Simple Sentences Workbook

This book is made just for YOU — a young writer ready to learn, laugh, and create. Whether you're just starting to write letters or already making full sentences, Penelope the Pencil and her friends will guide you every step of the way. Inside, you'll meet a fun group of writing tools — like Carl the Crayon, Mia the Marker, Ernie the Eraser, and Sally the Sharpener.

Together, they'll help you:

Write your name
Learn new words
Build strong sentences
Create your very own stories

You'll trace, write, draw, and imagine your way through various pages of handwriting fun. Don't worry about mistakes — even Ernie the Eraser says, "It's okay to try again!"
So grab your pencil and let's begin your writing adventure!

Let's write the world your way!

Penelope the Pencil loves to write.
She writes every day and every night.

"I can write my name!" says Penelope.

Penelope
____

Trace over Penelope's name.

Can you write your name? Let's see!

My name is: _______________________.

Now trace: My name is

Now write the complete sentence using the lines below.

Penelope looks around.
She sees her desk, her books, and her backpack.

"I can write what I see!" she says.

Trace over the items that Penelope sees.

Write three items that you see.

I see a _______________________.

I see a _______________________.

I see a _______________________.

Now write the complete sentences using the lines below.

Penelope has a new plan.

"I will write small words!" she says.
She picks up her pencil and starts to think.

She writes: Cat

Then she writes: Dog

And then: Sun

Trace over the words cat, dog, and sun.

"I can write sentences using small words!" Penelope exclaims.

Penelope writes a sentence: The cat runs.

Next she writes: The dog barks.

Then she writes: The sun is bright.

Trace over the sentences.

Now write the complete sentences using the lines below.

Now it's your turn! Write three small words.

1. ______________________________

2. ______________________________

3. ______________________________

Practice writing the words below.

Now try using the words in complete sentences.

Penelope sees her friend Carl the Crayon.

"Hi, Penelope!" he says.

"Let's write rhyming words!"

Trace over the rhyming words.

hat fun big lap sad like

sat run dig map mad hike

mat bun pig cap had bike

Trace the sentence starters and fill in the blanks using the rhyming words you just traced.

I like to ________________.

I sat on the ________________.

I ride my ________________.

Now write the complete sentences using the lines below.

"Let's write more words that rhyme, Penelope." says Carl.

Carl writes: make

Penelope writes: bake

They both write: cake

Trace over the words.

Now write the words using the lines below.

Trace the sentence starters and fill in the blanks using the rhyming words make, bake, and cake.

Let's _________________________ a treat.

We can _________________________ something sweet.

A delicious _________________________ to eat.

Now write the complete sentences using the lines below.

Trace the rhyming sentences.

I like to run for fun.
The frog sat on a log.
The cat laid on the mat.

Now write the complete sentences using the lines below.

Trace the rhyming sentences.

Sal is my best pal.
The pig loves to dig.
I saw the ball fall.

Now write the complete sentences using the lines below.

Now it's your turn! Write three rhyming words.

1. ________________________

2. ________________________

3. ________________________

Practice writing the words below.

Now try using the words in complete sentences.

Adjectives are words that describe. Trace over the adjectives.

pretty fluffy smart sunny angry

handsome delicious perfect tiny

amazing large rough juicy silly

Trace over the adjectives below.

Trace over the adjectives below.

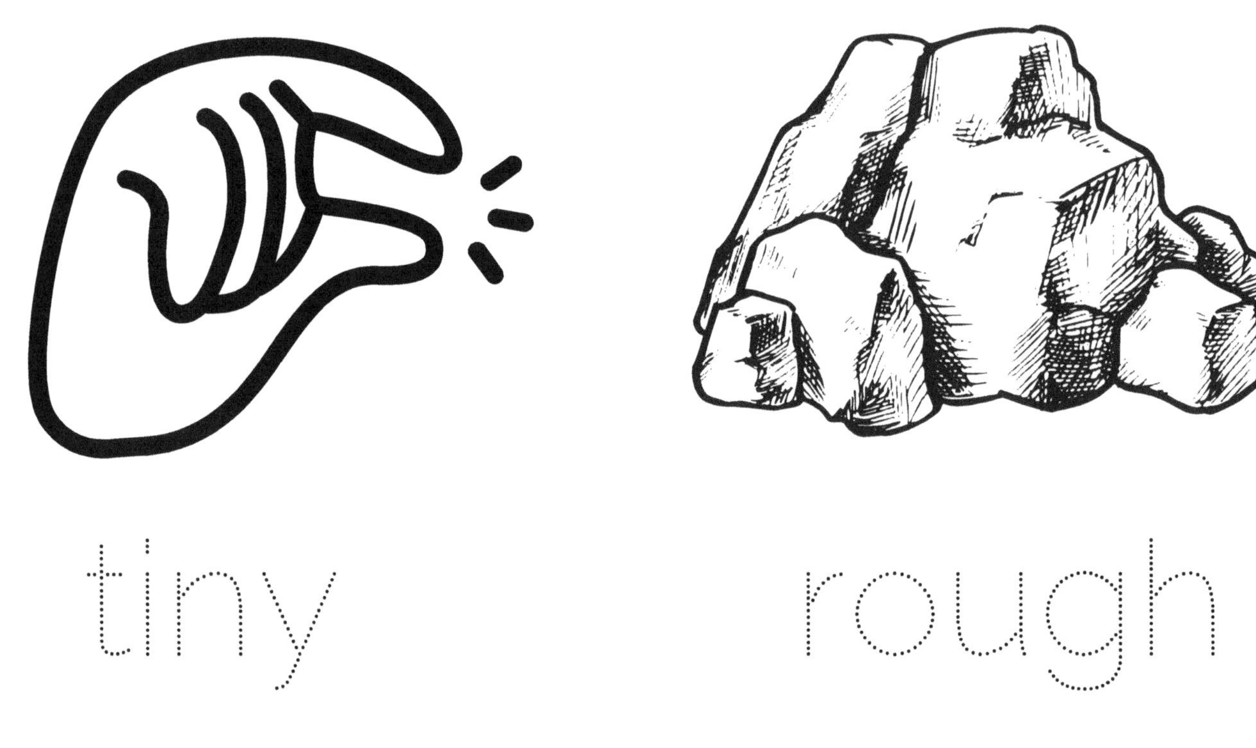

tiny

rough

delicious

pretty

Trace the sentence starters and fill in the blanks using the adjectives you just traced.

The flower is ___________________.

The apple is ___________________.

The mouse is ___________________.

Now write the complete sentences using the lines below.

"Let's write more adjectives, Penelope and Carl." says Mia.

Mia writes: funny

Penelope writes: tasty

Carl writes: bouncy

Trace over the words.

Now write the words using the lines below.

Trace the sentence starters and fill in the blanks using the adjectives funny, tasty, and bouncy.

The clown is ________________________.

The food is ________________________.

The ball is ________________________.

Now write the complete sentences using the lines below.

Trace the sentences.

The peach is ripe and juicy.
The tree is gigantic.
The chips are crunchy.

Now write the complete sentences using the lines below.

Trace the sentences.

The apple is red and shiny.
The pancakes are fluffy.
The sky is clear and blue.

Now write the complete sentences using the lines below.

Now it's your turn! Write three adjectives.

1. ______________________________

2. ______________________________

3. ______________________________

Practice writing the words below.

Now try using the words in complete sentences.

Verbs are action words. Trace over the verbs below.

walk   hop   skip   paint   dance

drink   sleep   play   push   build

pull   drive   catch   draw   cook

Trace over the verbs below.

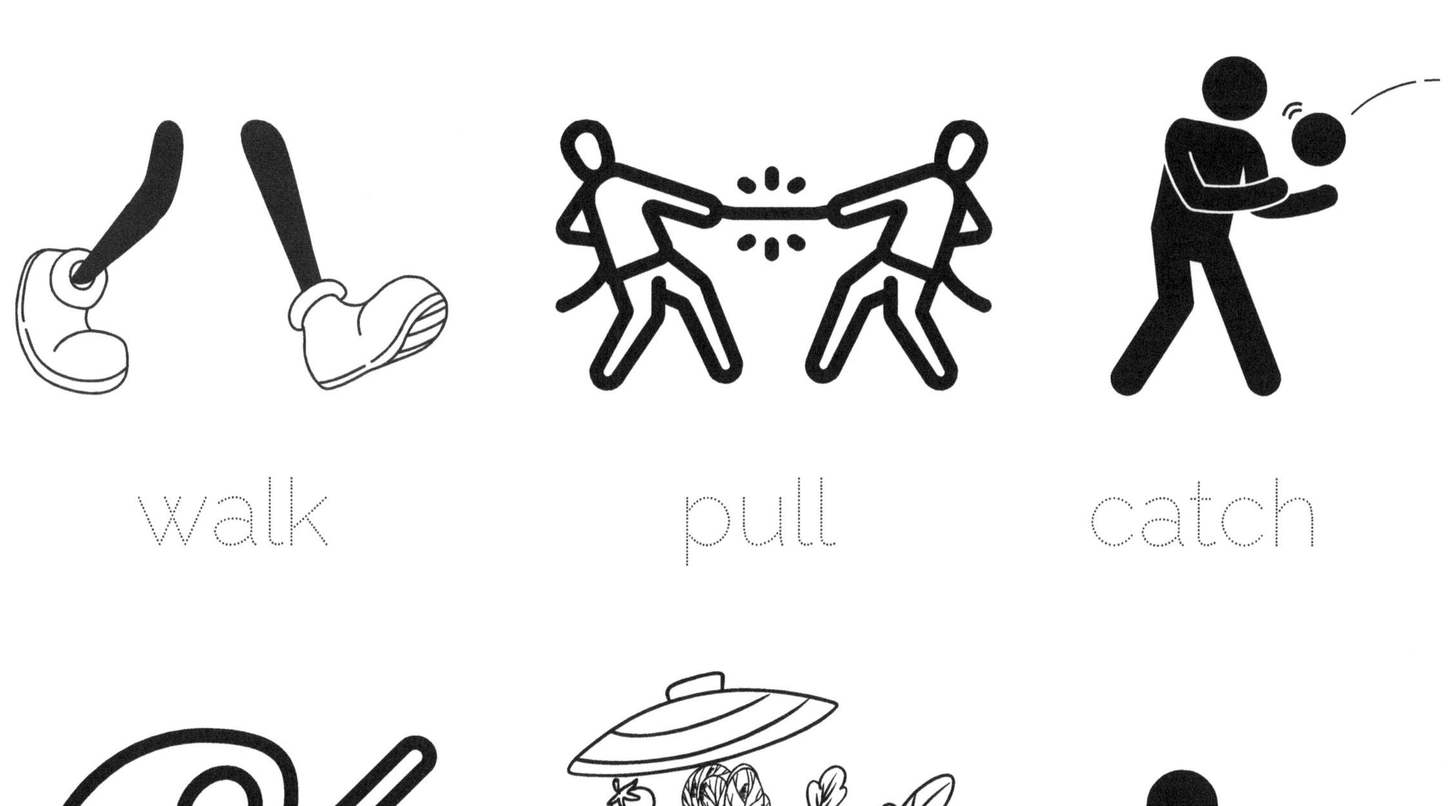

Trace the sentence starters and fill in the blanks using the verbs you just traced.

The frog likes to ___________________________.

The kids like to ___________________________.

The artist loves to ___________________________.

Now write the complete sentences using the lines below.

"Writing verbs is fun, let's write some more!" says Ernie.

Ernie writes: leap

Next Ernie writes: jump

Then Ernie writes: create

Trace over the words.

Now write the words using the lines below.

Trace the sentences.

Now write the complete sentences using the lines below.

Trace the sentences.

Susie likes to cook .

Adam chose to paint.

Timmy went to sleep.

Now write the complete sentences using the lines below.

Now it's your turn! Write three verbs.

1. ___________________________

2. ___________________________

3. ___________________________

Practice writing the words below.

Now try using the words in complete sentences.

Trace over the sentences below & rewrite them.

We go to the park.

We run and play.

We laugh all day.

Trace the sentence starters and fill in the blanks.

We go to the _______________________.

We _______________________.

We _______________________.

Now write the complete sentences using the lines below.

Let's write some more! Trace the sentence starters and fill in the blanks.

Next we ___________________________.

Then we ___________________________.

Finally we ___________________________.

Now write the complete sentences using the lines below.

"Even if you make a mistake, it's okay." says Ernie.

"We can always try again!" exclaims Penelope.

"Writers keep writing!"

Don't worry about being perfect. Just try your best! Let's practice writing again. Trace over the sentences below and rewrite them.

I went to the store.

____

I bought snacks.

____

Then I went home.

____

"I'm ready for a story!" Mia says.
"Let's use our words and make a beginning, middle, and end!"

"Every story starts with an idea." Carl expresses.
"What will our story be about?"
"Let's write a story about a lost puppy!" Mia suggests.

Continue writing the story with the sentence starter below.

One day, a precious puppy

got lost on his way home.

Use the space to illustrate a picture.

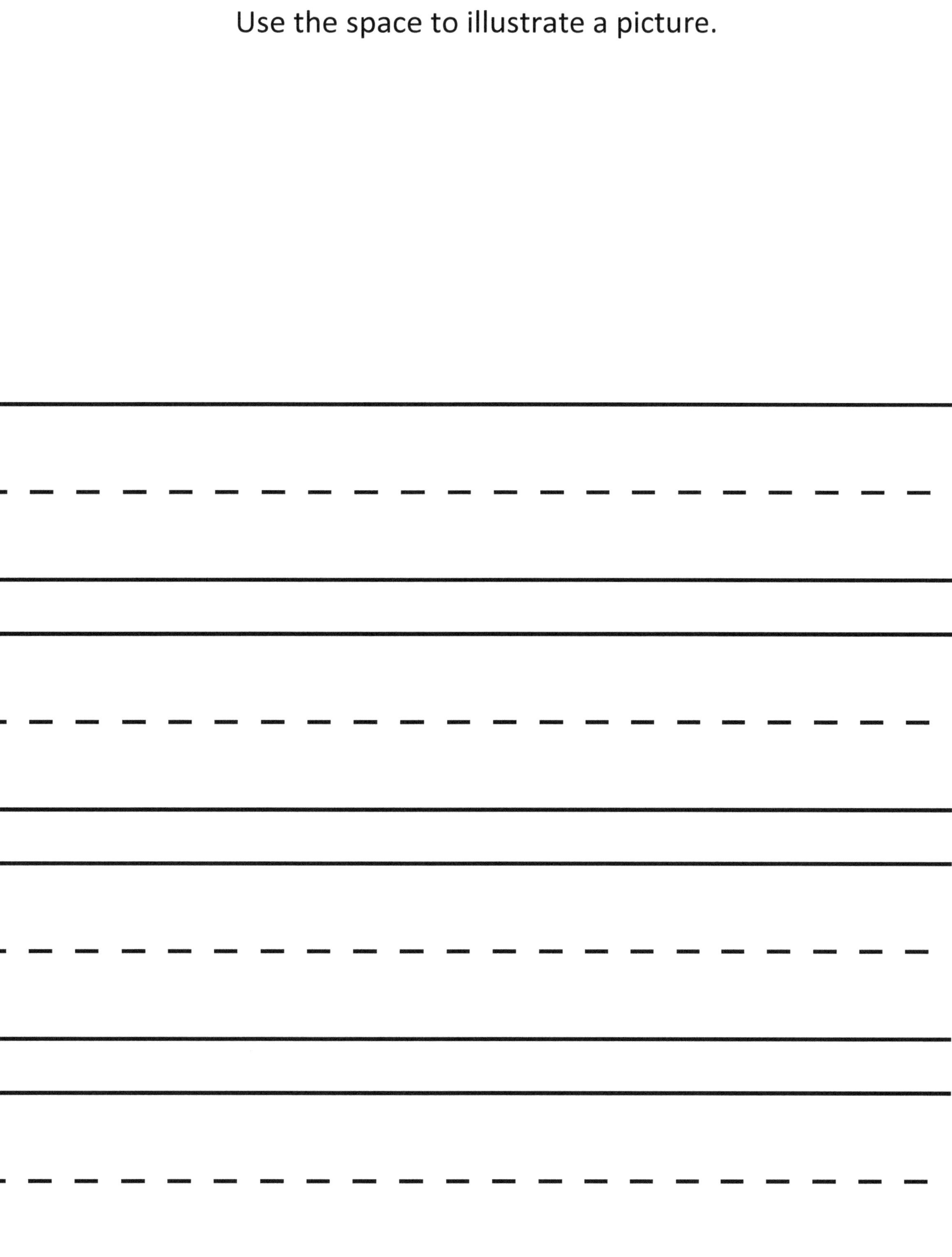

"Continue writing the story and add that the puppy finds a friend." says Sally.

Penelope writes the middle.

Continue writing the story with the sentence starter below.

Along his journey, the

puppy found a friend.

Use the space to illustrate a picture.

Continue writing the story with the sentence starter below.

The puppy and his new friend

worked together.

Use the space to illustrate a picture.

Penelope says, "Let's try a silly story!"

Trace over the sentences below & rewrite them.

A cat wears a hat.

The cat flies a kite.

The hat falls off in the wind.

What will your silly story be?

____

____

Who are the characters?

____

____

What silly thing happens?

____

____

How does it end?

____

____

Now it's time to write your silly story all on your own!
Be sure to draw illustrations.

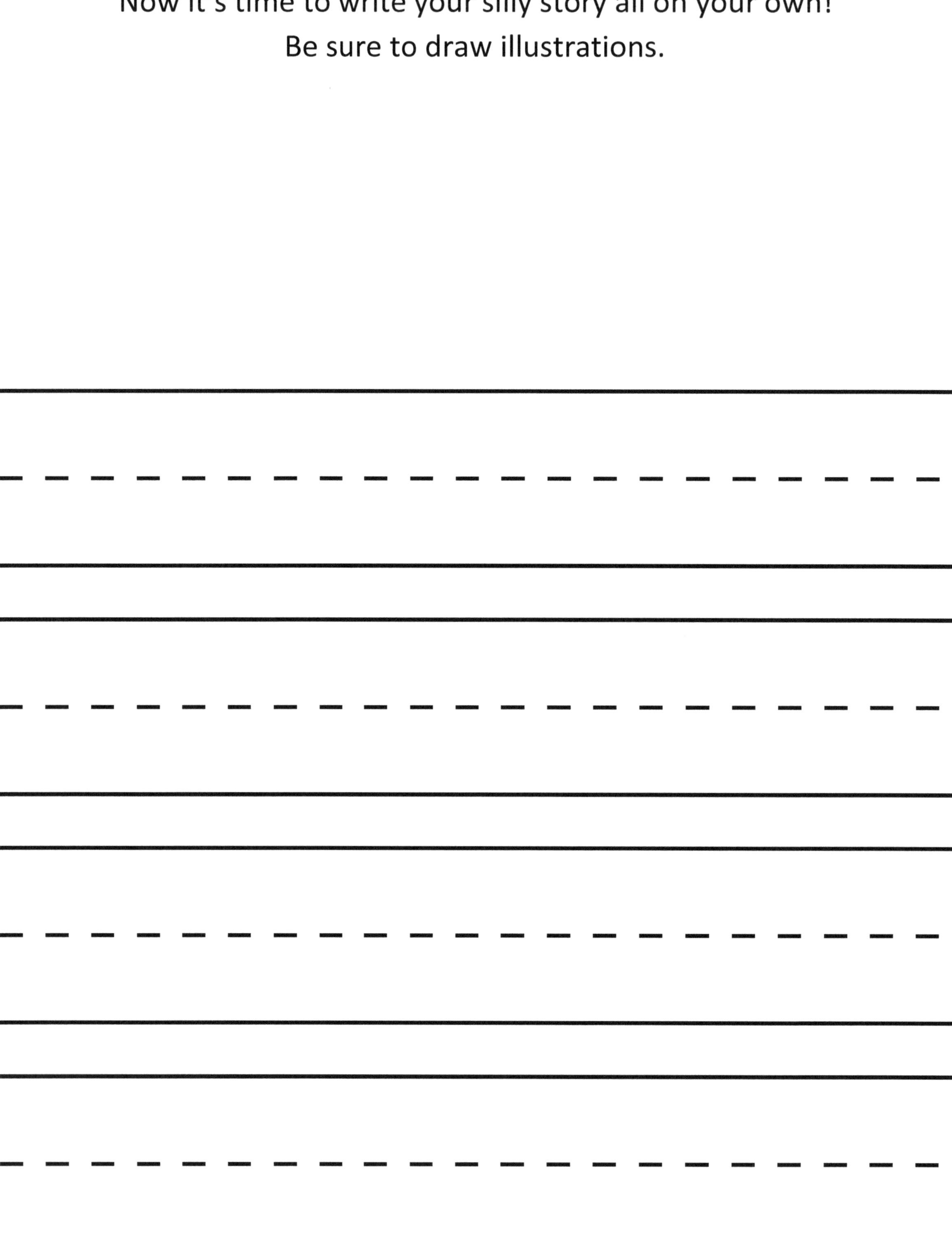

Penelope the Pencil, Carl the Crayon,
Mia the Marker, Ernie the Eraser,
and Sally the Sharpener
all CHEER!

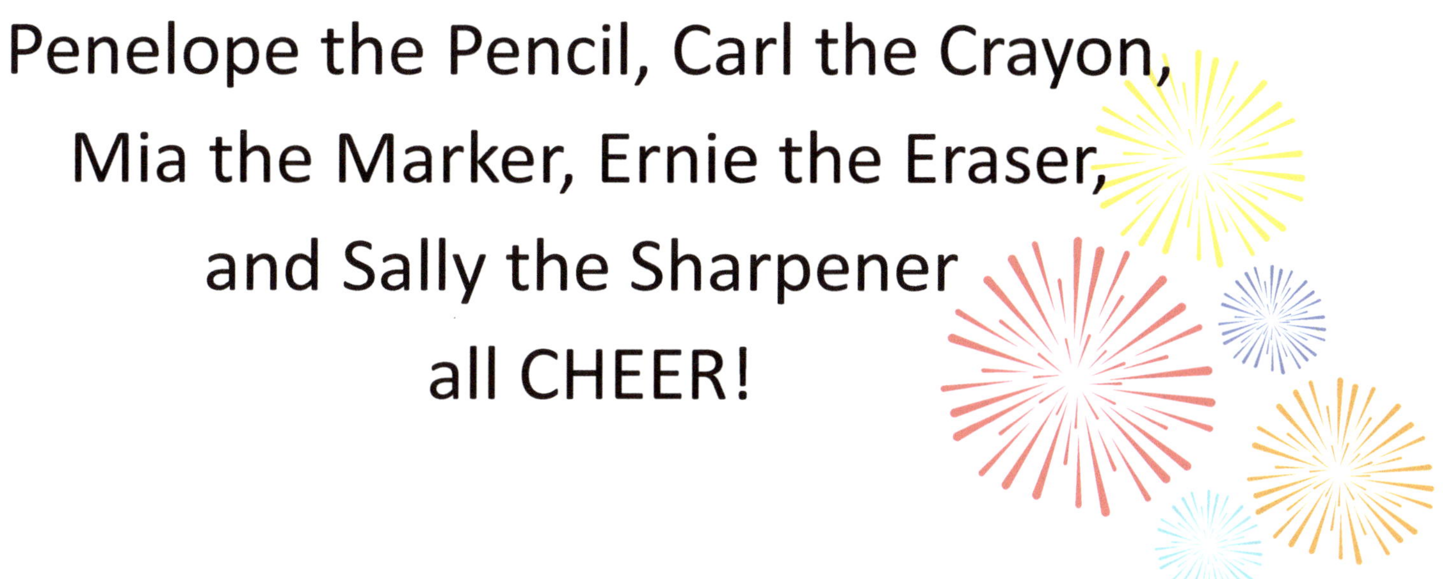

"You did it!"
"You learned to write your name, new
words, sentences,
and your very own stories!"

What do you want to write next?

- ☐ A story about an animal
- ☐ A letter to a friend
- ☐ A silly poem
- ☐ A journal about my day
- ☐ Something else:

____

My writing goal is:

I want to write

____

WRITING PRACTICE

Use the blank pages
to write and
illustrate.

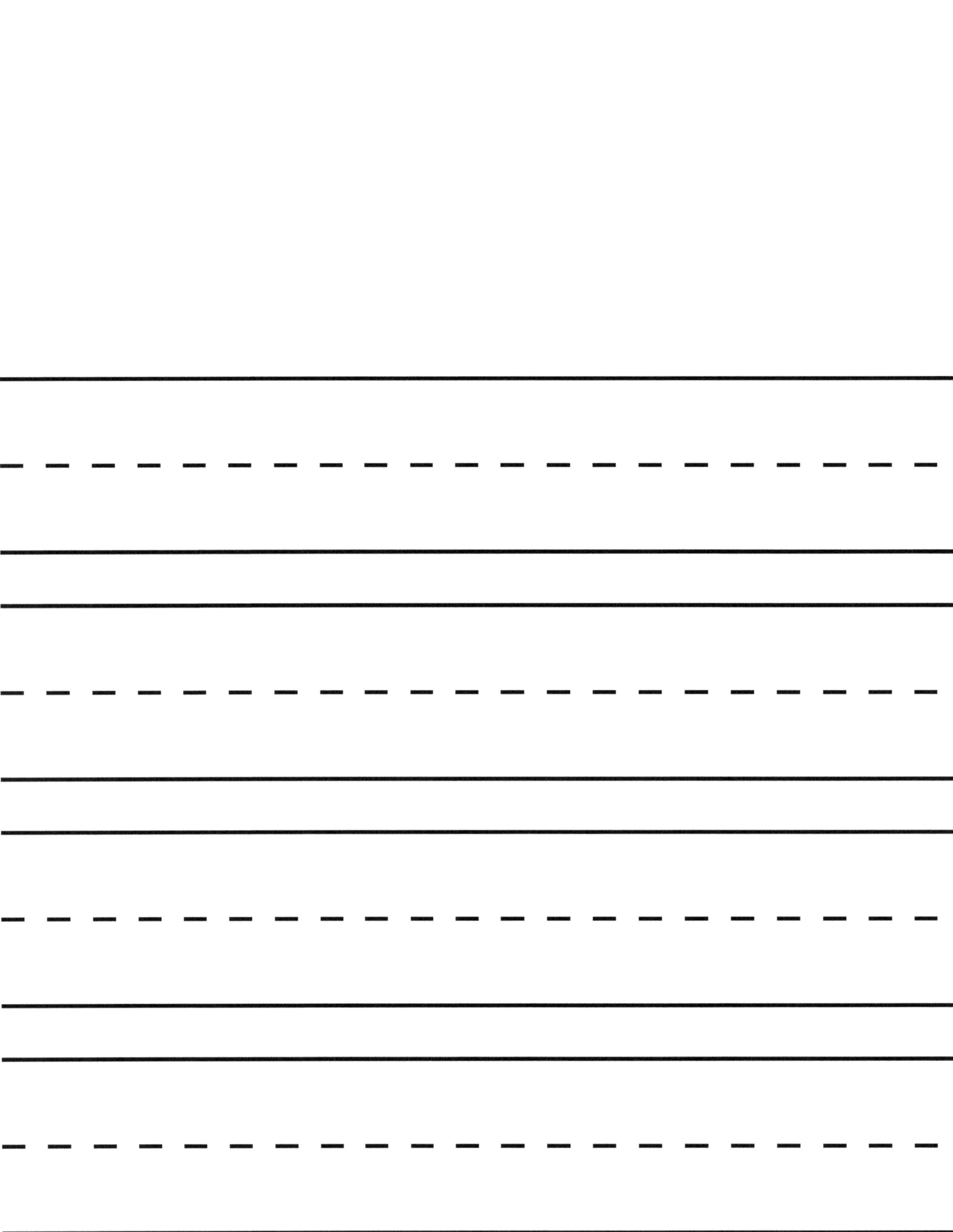

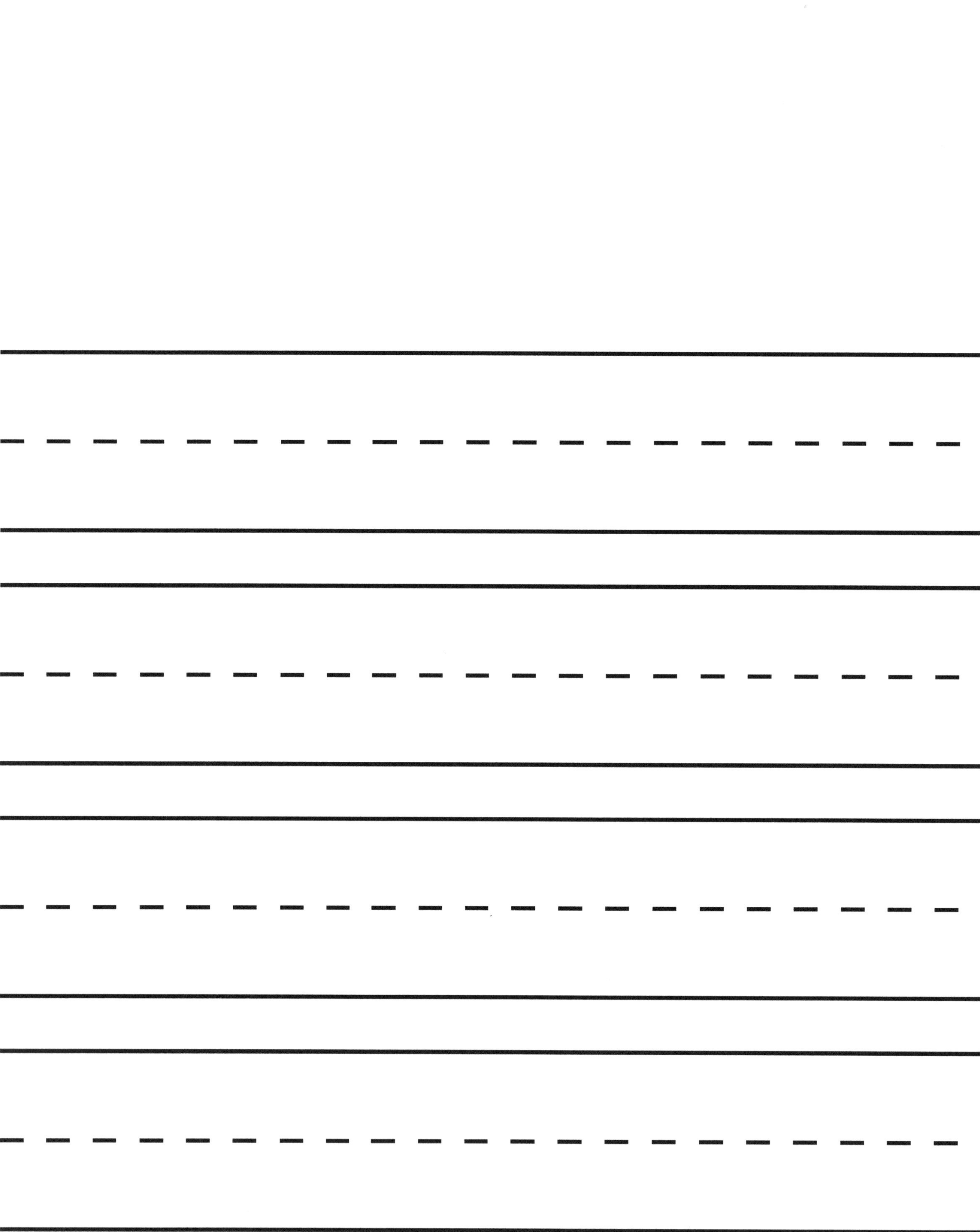

WRITER'S CERTIFICATE

This certifies that

---

is an amazing writer.

Keep writing, dreaming, and creating.

Date:

---

www.ingramcontent.com/pod-product-compliance
Lightning Source LLC
Chambersburg PA
CBHW041602110726
48005CB00002B/261